Author's Note:

The character Aroma is presented as the one who draws her way through the book, although I haven't included an image that shows her doing this. Instead, I show her interacting with the pictures that she sees herself in as she begins to realise that there is greater meaning to them than she first thought.

First Published in 2018 by Shortbread and Penny Sweet Publishing UK

shortbreadandpennysweetpublish@gmail.com

Copyright ©2018 by Tamara Anthony

This book was created in coloured pencil and tempera.

First Edition

ISBN 978-0995718012

Edited by Shortbread and Penny Sweet Publishing

Beyond The Mirror

Written and Illustrated

By

Tamara Anthony

The King had given Aroma the gift of drawing and although she had already begun to use it, there was something more for her to do and see.

The King was invisible to the natural eye and so to see Him Aroma had to look into the eternal book which was likened to looking into a mirror. This was the place where she would see and find everything she needed, for it was here that she would find her true self and it was here that His Kingdom would be revealed to her.

It was therefore no ordinary mirror, so she wanted to look further. And then a thought crossed her mind that perhaps she was to go through the mirror instead.

Well of course she couldn't physically go through, but she could use her gift to draw her way instead.

In fact, Aroma had long been searching for a secret doorway that would lead to a place beyond. She had previously pictured in her mind an old cupboard which led to a storehouse full of gifts; however, there was something special about her drawing gift and more importantly, there was something very special about the mirror.

So she began to climb through.

Half in half out she sat on the bottom edge of the frame because there was no where to put her foot and below was a very steep drop.

In fact, she didn't want to go any further just yet, for it hadn't even occurred to her that she could despite the fact that she could draw it. She had forgotten about that.

So there was nothing to stop her, except that she hadn't drawn in this way before. She wasn't sure where it would lead or what the meanings were of the pictures that came to her mind. She wasn't sure how real they were because these things weren't seen with the natural eye. She also knew that she wouldn't see anything if she didn't take the time to look.

However, disappointingly, she sat looking into what seemed to be an old, wooden attic which wasn't what she had hoped for or expected: there was nothing glorious about an attic and where the King lived was supposed to be glorious.

Nevertheless, she had no choice but to draw what she saw, and as she began she found herself colouring the brown wood blue. She had to colour it blue because she believed that colours had meaning and blue meant grace. It was grace that brought the glorious blessings of the Kingdom into reality and she also knew that the King's book gave clear instructions to go boldly into the throne room to find it.

But it wasn't just for her.

Her best friend, Chuku, stood peering over: 'Where are the others?' he asked, having already asked the same question on another occasion.

Well, she supposed that he made a good point because Aroma always seemed to be on her own. Maybe her adventure in picture books would be more interesting with other people in them, but who was like her; she felt so different from everyone else; yet there *were* others.

For now though, she drew him in the picture because he was in it already; if he was with her, then he was in it and she wanted him to be with her on this journey too. So she drew him beside her whilst wondering where it would lead and if this was the beginning of something so much greater.

In one sense the journey would be even more interesting if she were to include other people, especially if she were to draw them and their responses to the pictures too. What's more, for the fact that Aroma was even wondering there had to be an answer and she knew that the King would reveal this to her.

And as it happened Aroma showed Rise and Gloria the picture, and the three of them peered through the mirror at the same time they looked at the drawing of the browny-blue room.

'That looks scary,' said Rise with a slightly disturbed expression.

'Oh dear,' thought Aroma agreeably because it did look scary and she didn't know where she was going just yet.

'Wait a minute,' said Gloria. 'This is Aroma's mind. She hasn't seen this before; none of us have, but look at the darkness, it's the unknown and it is clearing. It seems scary *and* disappointing at first but only to the natural mind. This shows the renewing of the mind to the things not yet seen or known; remember what it says in the King's book,' she said encouragingly.

Phew! Aroma thought, quite relieved.

So there she was in the picture still sat on the edge not quite ready to go further; drawing took time and there were other things she had to do before she could draw the next step.

Then,

finally she jumped…

...right into what looked like a tall panelled building.

Well, she hadn't seen anything like this before, but then she remembered the words in the King's book that said that He was a 'strong tower' and that this was a safe place to be.

However, knowing this really wasn't any comfort to her at that point because it looked like nothing was in it; to her this meant there was nothing to do or see and she didn't know how she could possibly stay or if she was supposed to.

'What's in here?' she asked as she looked down at herself in the picture she had just drawn.

And as she looked, way above her head she could see the words 'NO LIMITS' written in white.

But what did that really mean?

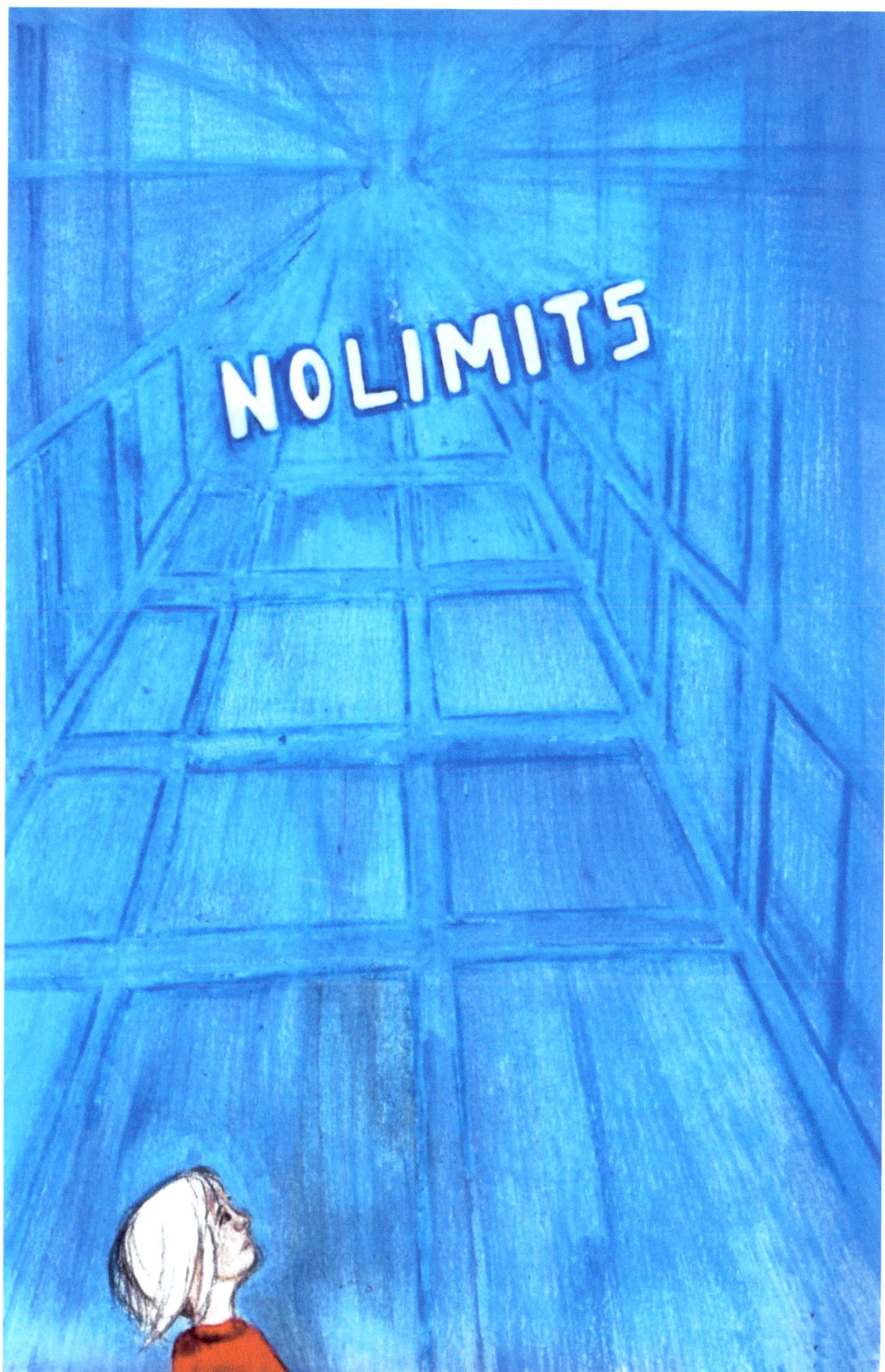

She tried to see if she could push her way out through the walls. She knocked and she pulled at the sides like they were cloth. She wanted to do something or go somewhere and she was slightly panicked; but you see, she couldn't do anything or go anywhere for it would only be a waste of time and energy.

'How do l get back? There's nothing in here,' she called out.

'You don't!' He replied softly. 'Not unless you really want to.'

But Aroma continued with her thoughts as if He hadn't spoken because she didn't understand and she felt unsettled. She was finding it hard to take the King seriously. In fact, she didn't even know if it was her voice or His.

'Be free.' He said.

Well, she didn't know what freedom was, not really anyway.

What happens now? Aroma asked
with an even louder voice.

MIRACLES SIGNS & WONDERS

... He replied.

But she couldn't stay any longer for she had run out of time.

So she climbed back into her room where it was much more comfortable.

Yet strange as it was, she was in two places at the same time, but she wasn't sure what that really meant or how she was to draw it.

And then a few days later, as she lay with her eyes closed, a picture appeared in her mind.

©AROMA 16

Now she was being shown something much greater, since there had to be a reason why there were now two mirrors; so she drew herself sat between them wondering what that could be.

She knew that the first mirror was eternal and what lay on the other side of it was hidden to many; however, the second mirror was broken and showed a brick wall that didn't reflect back anything, not even herself. It was as if she no longer existed although, she knew that the physical world had to reflect the Kingdom: the physical had to be changed by what lay hidden beyond the eternal mirror and there was no reflection of herself anymore in the broken one.

Yet as she continued to ponder she could also see that the two mirrors showed the difference between limit and no limits. Living from no limits was the truth of her position in the King's Kingdom and this was where she was to stay. But it was difficult. How could she do that?

Moreover, it was the difference between truth and lies; the known and the unknown; the power of grace instead of her efforts and there was a choice that everyone had to make and Aroma could see this. But she wasn't sure how to draw it because she wasn't sure that she had fully experienced or taken hold of this truth, or indeed if she had really accepted it.

So she walked
away from the
two mirrors.

But there was
nowhere else to
go.

She had to go
back to the
eternal mirror
because this was
the only place
she would find
the answers.

So she stared into the blue room again.

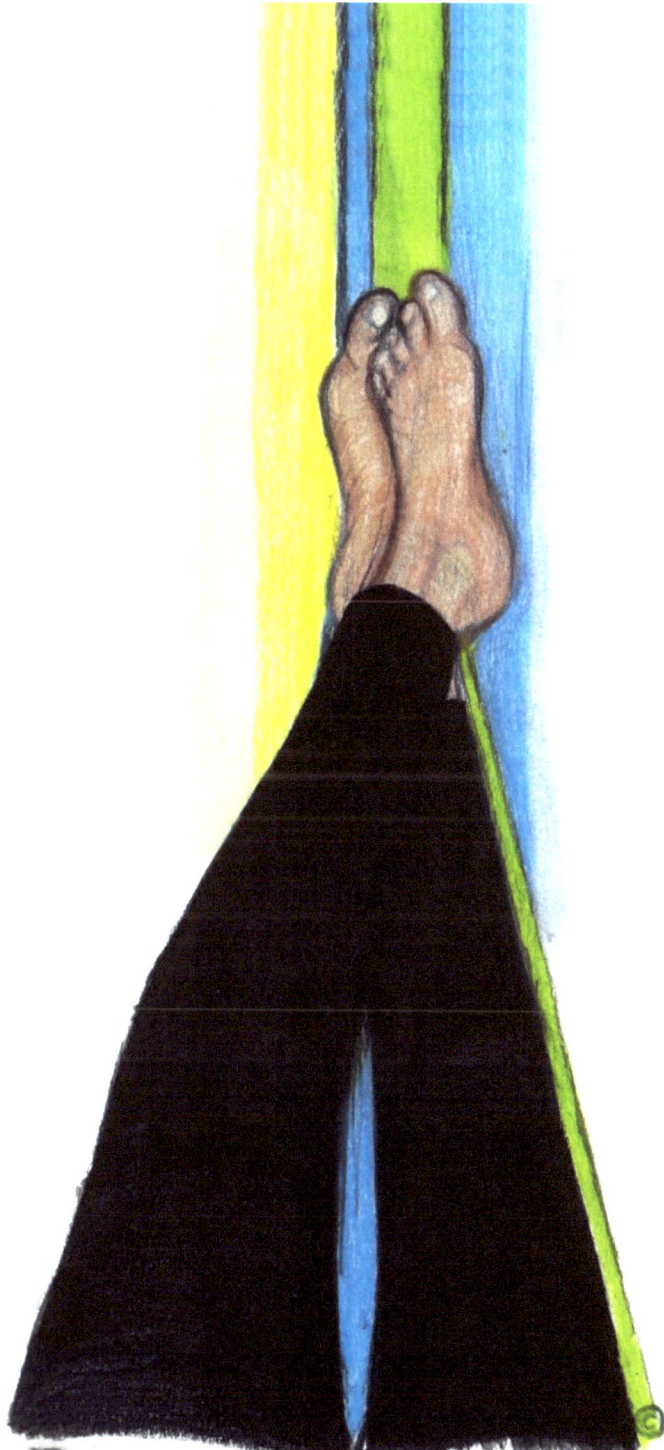

And she continued to ponder when she then looked down at the image she had just drawn.

And there she was between two realms.

And now she understood that in the blue room there was nothing for her to do and that it was where miracles, signs and wonders would take place; but she didn't know how except that it was by the Spirit.

Was grace the King's Spirit then? She wondered.

Was she to put this blue grace on her like clothes, meaning the Spirit?

Or was grace inside of her, just like her King; He was full of grace and truth and He was full of the Spirit. But was she?

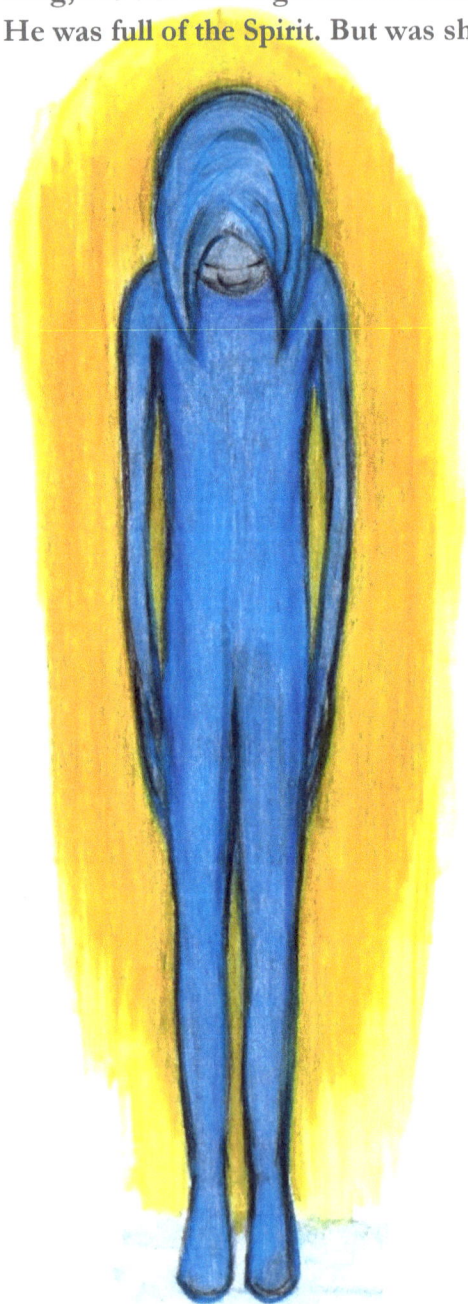

She knew her body was visible
and physical and the Spirit,
spiritual. 'That's it,' she
thought. 'This must mean
being in two places at once.'

Was the Spirit inside the whole of her like molecules, and was He full in her?

'How is Your power released Lord?' She asked the King.

'By My Spirit: by believing in Me; by relying on My life in you; by taking hold of the truth of my grace; Just ask and rest in knowing this truth and see what happens.' He replied.

'Oh.' she answered. 'You work with my spirit and soul.

My soul: through my mind; what I think; what I choose and through my emotions. The soul is to rest and wait on You as You are revealed outwardly through my body.' She realised.

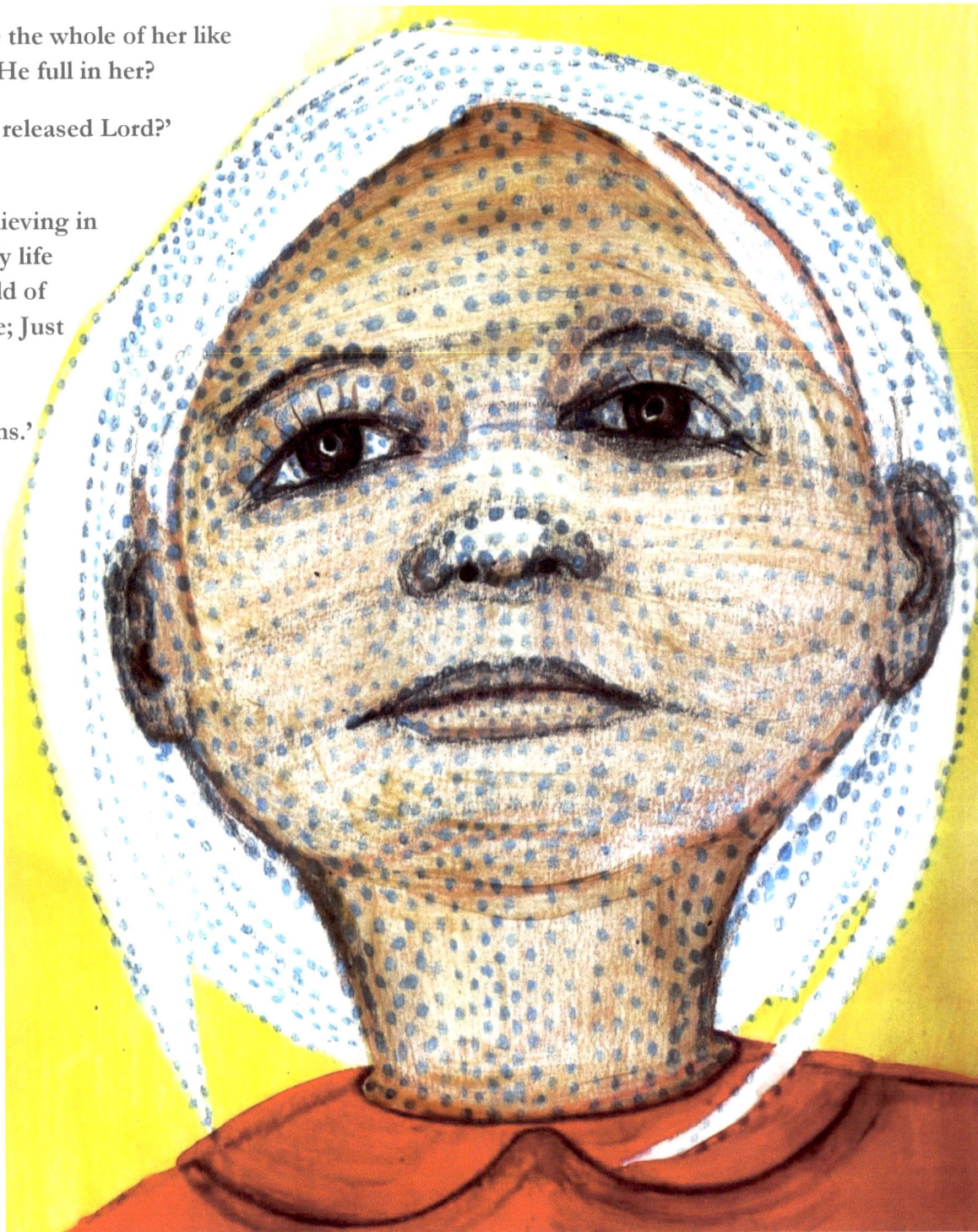

And at the same time she was beginning to understand this she was also taken to the place that revealed this in His book: that His Spirit is the Spirit of grace that lives inside the King and now works through her.

So she decided to draw Him to look like herself despite the fact that He was known as He; after all, He lived in her too; although she knew she needed to know and understand how they were supposed to work together.

So she continued to draw.

Now then, was it that she was supposed to be behind Him allowing Him to lead the way?

She knew that even if this was the case it didn't always happen.

Or, was she a small person carried by Him as a spectator sitting on His shoulder? Was this what it was like living with the Spirit?

She had already experienced seeing things happen that were beyond her control just as if she really were only watching.

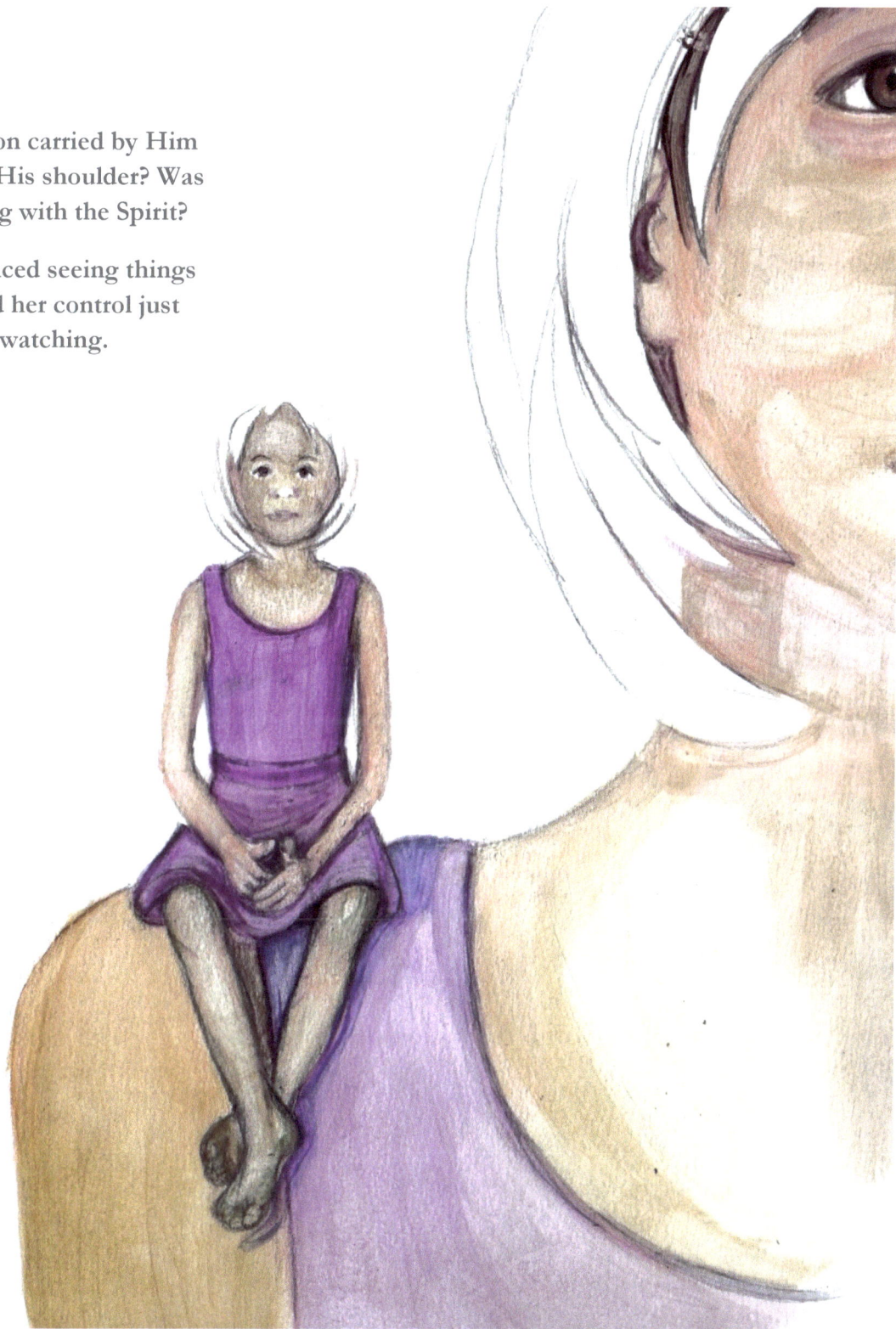

Or was she consumed by Him as in jumping into Him like jumping through the eternal mirror into His grace, but inside of her?

Or was it the other way round: inside out, or both?

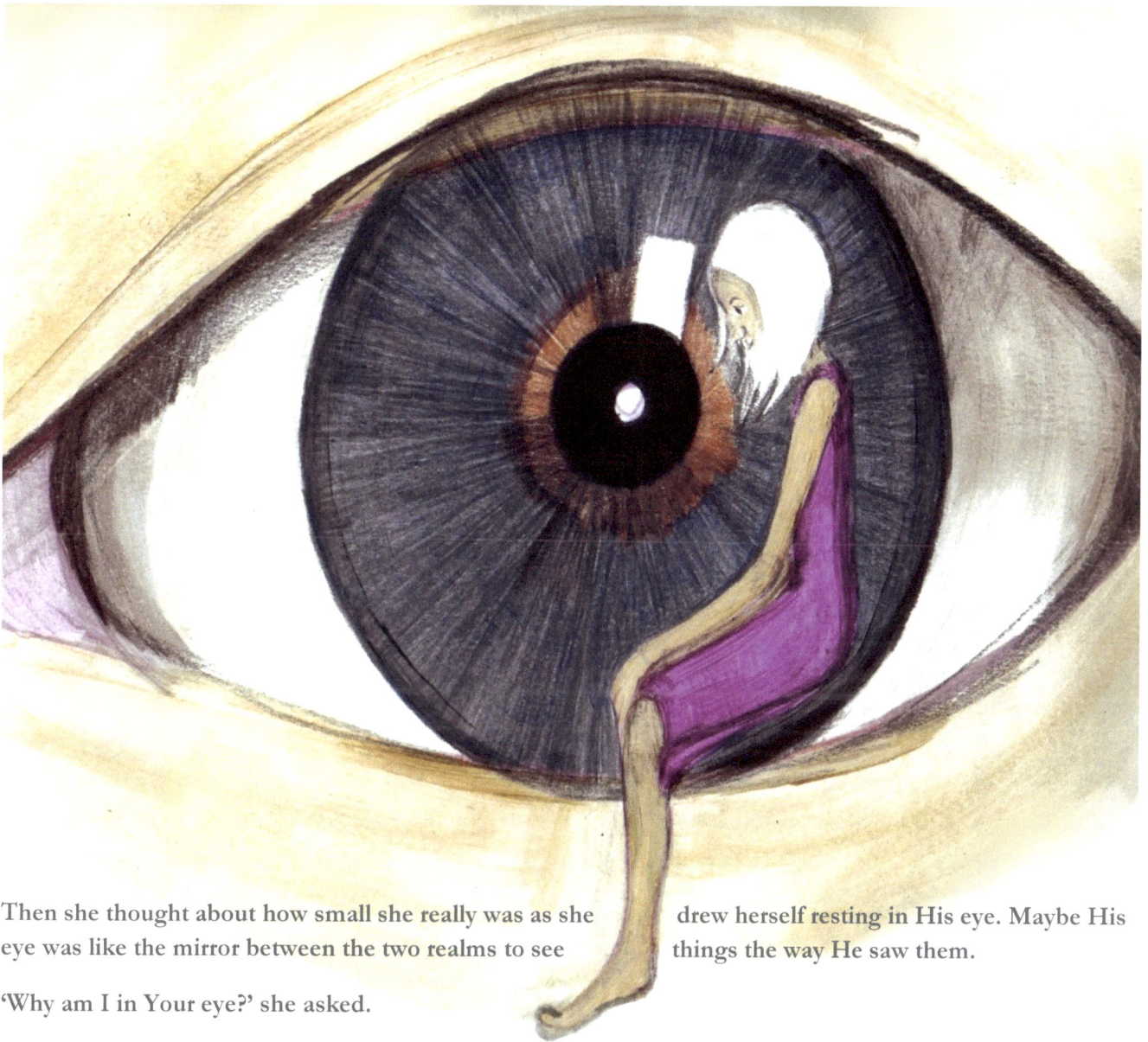

Then she thought about how small she really was as she drew herself resting in His eye. Maybe His eye was like the mirror between the two realms to see things the way He saw them.

'Why am I in Your eye?' she asked.

'You are the object of My affection and the apple of My eye. My grace is on you, around you and in you,' He said.

Then she remembered that Esther found grace in the King's sight and Noah also found grace in the eyes of the Lord. However, there was more to this than that, and as she thought about it, she realised that His eyes must be on her all the time. And again, mysteriously He showed her this truth in His book.

Yet even though she was beginning to learn what it meant to be in His eyes, she continued to wrestle and battle and tried to apply her mind to everything that she had seen so far:

'Who are You really Holy Spirit?' she asked. 'What does it mean to live in You? Where are You, What do You do? What does it mean that You can be full in me and take over? How can You do this?' she continued. 'I'm scared I can't let go of things. I am scared I will have to do something and I'm afraid that I can't.'

Then she realised that she wasn't always aware that when she couldn't do something it was because she was thinking that He wasn't enough and that she had to try to do it because it wasn't happening the way she thought it should. And then again she realised that this was wrong thinking because His grace was sufficient for what He wanted to do through her; it had to be and she just had to let Him.

Was this what He meant by freedom: to rest in Him and trust in His Spirit of power in grace and truth as He operated through her soul. That was the only thing she was to do: to acknowledge her true position; to ask Him and keep on asking; to allow Him; to rest in Him and trust and depend on Him, for His grace would be given for what was needed.

Then something amazing happened: She realised and experienced His power. *Now* she was beginning to understand what it meant to let Him. It was like floating in the blue room of trust in His grace as He worked through her soul; and maybe this was what it meant to be in His eye: hidden in Him, yet seeing things happen as He saw them.

It was an experience like nothing she had ever known before. But it was also a continual submission to Him, which only really began when she saw the reality of what was on the other side of the mirror in living in the realm of the Kingdom in Him. And He had always been there, ever since she first believed that there really was a King beyond this world and that out of her would flow His Spirit of grace. Although she knew she had to continually give up wrestling and accept that this is what it meant to live in two places at once: in dependence on His Spirit.

So is this the end of the story?

Well, yes, but at the same time it can only be the beginning, for little did she know that she would have to remember again and again that this was where she really belonged.

No wonder she drew His eye, for He was going to let her see so much more!

Other Books:

The Perfect Gift

ISBN: 978-0995718005

The
Perfect
Gift

Written and Illustrated by
Tatiana Andreou

www.ingramcontent.com/pod-product-compliance
Lightning Source LLC
Chambersburg PA
CBHW042114040426

42448CB00003B/273